in
the
news™

OUTSOURCING
U.S. JOBS

Jacqueline Ching

ROSEN
PUBLISHING®

New York

For Prentis

Published in 2009 by The Rosen Publishing Group, Inc.
29 East 21st Street, New York, NY 10010

Copyright © 2009 by The Rosen Publishing Group, Inc.

First Edition

Library of Congress Cataloging-in-Publication Data

Ching, Jacqueline.
Outsourcing U.S. jobs / Jacqueline Ching.
    p. cm. — (In the news)
Includes bibliographical references and index.
ISBN-13: 978-1-4358-5039-2 (library binding)
ISBN-13: 978-1-4358-5367-6 (pbk)
ISBN-13: 978-1-4358-5373-7 (6 pack)
1. Contracting out—United States. 2. Labor market—United States. I. Title.
HD2365.C465 2009
331.13—dc22

2008016890

Manufactured in Malaysia

On the cover: Clockwise from top left: An international gathering of
trade and economics officials discusses issues related to globalization,
free trade, and outsourcing; an American contact lens cleaner company's
call center in the Philippines; an auto parts factory that has been shut
down stands behind locked gates in Dayton, Ohio.

contents

Outsourcing: A Modern Business Strategy

T he board game Monopoly is the first experience that most of us have with the world of business. In Monopoly, the goal is to do whatever you have to in order to increase your wealth, including buying properties, charging rent, and negotiating and trading with your opponents.

In real life, companies are formed to earn profits and increase the wealth of their owners. They have to continuously think of innovative ways to outdo their competitors. Gaining a competitive edge could mean any number of things: creating a better product or service, offering it at a lower cost, creating stronger brand recognition, or a combination of these, and more. To achieve these goals, companies analyze the different facets of their business—manufacturing, accounting, human resources, warehousing, transportation, customer service, and information technology (IT) management, for example. They then come up with strategies to make each of these more efficient and cost effective.

In Monopoly, players negotiate with each other with the goal of increasing their wealth, just as real businesses do.

The Ins and Outs of Outsourcing

Outsourcing is simply a business strategy whereby a company pays an outside service provider (a person or company) to do a job that would normally be performed by its own staff. The service provider, or contractor, can be located in the same country as the business. But most people associate the term "outsourcing" with providers that are located in foreign countries. Because outsourcing is a global phenomenon, it gives companies a vast range of options from which to choose. Companies have found it to be a way to reduce costs, become more efficient, and compete in a global economy.

Many jobs that are not considered core to a company can be outsourced. For example, a company that manufactures automobiles may choose to outsource its accounting needs. This frees it to use its extra capital and resources on its core activities, which are related to actually making the cars. When you make an online purchase, the product has to be collected from a storage facility and shipped to you. The job of fulfilling and shipping orders that are received online is called online fulfillment. Many companies look to outside parties to handle this instead of building and operating their own warehouse and managing a fleet of airplanes or trucks.

U.S. companies also turn to outsourcing as a way to carry on with after-hours business, when most American workers are asleep. Customer call centers, software troubleshooting, and even medical diagnoses can be handled on a twenty-four-hour basis overseas in countries such as India and the Philippines. Globalization makes the location of workers performing many jobs irrelevant.

Outsourcing doesn't necessarily mean sending jobs overseas, although it has become synonymous with this. It can be as simple as a company hiring an accounting firm to handle its tax filings. Most companies outsource some part of their business operations or services. A better term for exporting jobs may be "offshoring," or "offshore outsourcing." Related terms include "onshore outsourcing," which refers to outsourcing within the company's own country; "nearshore outsourcing," which refers to outsourcing to a neighboring country; and "insourcing," which simply means delegating jobs to a company's

When there was a shortage of U.S. radiologists and an exploding demand for more sophisticated scans to diagnose illnesses, the work was exported to places like India.

own staff. Third-party businesses are referred to as "suppliers," "vendors," "service providers," or "contractors." If individuals are providing the services, then they are called freelancers or consultants. From 2001 to 2006, American companies outsourced more than three million jobs to other countries.

In a single game of Monopoly, you have limited properties (those on the board, the plastic houses and hotels), limited trading partners (your fellow players), and limited functions (you can only buy properties and charge rent to increase your wealth). But imagine if there were fifty or a hundred games going on at once, each focused on a different way to make wealth, and it was possible to negotiate with players from any of those games. That's somewhat like the global market in which companies operate today.

When a company's executives decide to outsource, they must determine their objectives and then seek the approval of their board of directors, as they would when making any important strategic decision. Once the decision has been agreed upon, the company makes a request for proposals from a shortlist of suppliers. When the list is narrowed down to two or three contractors, there will be in-person interviews and perhaps a visit of their facilities. This is like a background check of the third party and may include interviews with the contractor's other customers and a review of its financial, legal, tax, and market situations. Then all the remaining contractors submit their "best and final offer." Lastly, a contract is signed with the winning contractor. An outsourcing arrangement defines how the client and contractor will work together and also covers services, a timeframe for when the contractor's services will begin and end, and privacy and security issues.

Globalization and Free Trade

The key concepts behind outsourcing are globalization and free trade. "Globalization" simply describes the current world economy, in which world markets are open to one another for trade, direct investment, flow of capital, and worker migration.

Global trade is nothing new. The economies of different countries have been open to each other throughout history to varying degrees. Notable examples include China's Silk Road, which opened up the trade route from China to the Mediterranean Sea as early as 114 BCE; Portugal's exploration and expansion into the New World in the sixteenth century; and the growth of trade between European powers, their colonies, and the United States in the nineteenth century. The word "globalization" first came into use in 1981. In the decades that followed, markets became increasingly open, especially with the spread of the Internet. Although outsourcing is nothing new, it is important to note that it has become a complex issue in today's global market.

"Free trade" refers to policies that allow the trade of goods and services to flow freely between nations. It is a market model that many believe helps companies to grow, maximize profits, and stimulate domestic economies.

After World War II, barriers to international trade were considerably lowered through international agreements negotiated under the General Agreement on Tariffs and Trade (GATT) treaty. In 1995, the World Trade Organization (WTO) was created to take over the

These seven members of the Appellate Body of the World Trade Organization (WTO) come from the Philippines, Egypt, Uruguay, the United States, New Zealand, Japan, and Germany.

functions of GATT, particularly the supervising and promoting of free trade. Liberal trade policies are what enable business activities such as outsourcing.

Today, all companies have to recognize that they are operating in a global environment. In order to compete, they cannot limit themselves only to resources found within the borders of their home country. They have to search the entire world for ideas, inspiration, resources, facilities, markets, consumers, and workers in order to gain and maintain a competitive edge.

The Evolution of Outsourcing

The first wave of modern outsourcing began in the 1980s with IT, a field that was growing rapidly. IT jobs encompass programming, computer services, and Internet services. The demand for IT workers who could develop software and hardware technologies ballooned. Strategies were put in place for companies to manage IT systems' maintenance, development, and application in-house. As the U.S. economy faltered, these companies had to seek lower-cost labor overseas, often in India, where a large, educated, and motivated workforce was willing and able to work for less than their American counterparts.

This was followed in the 1990s by a second wave of outsourcing service jobs, like billing, purchasing, customer service, and technical support. Companies expanded outside of India for their outsourcing needs to countries such as China, Canada, Argentina, and the Philippines.

The third and current wave of outsourcing is in the area of high-value knowledge-based services. These include everything that requires a high level of skill and creativity, including investment banking researchers, sales and marketing researchers, artists, writers, architects, scientists, high-end managers, planners and analysts, and health care and law professionals. According to Forrester Research, Inc., a technology and market research

The U.S. outsourcing industry in the Philippines grew from call centers but now includes legal services, Web design, medical transcription, software development, and animation.

company, by 2015, U.S. companies will outsource at least 3.3 million white-collar jobs to India, China, Pakistan, Vietnam, and Russia (many jobs are also outsourced to Europe, especially Eastern Europe). This translates to $136 billion in wages.

Reasons for Outsourcing

Outsourcing has become a commonplace practice, thanks to the growth of broadband Internet connections, improved shipping, open borders, increasing education, and the spread of English as a common language of business. India was one of the first countries to benefit from the outsourcing trend because it has a large population of English speakers and skilled workers, including a wealth of talented programmers.

It's hard to find a company that doesn't outsource at least some small part of its business. Forrester Research estimated that 40 percent of Fortune 1,000 companies use outsourcing as part of their business strategy. Companies that have moved jobs overseas include household names such as MCI, Verizon, Delta Airlines, Microsoft, Citigroup, Hewlett Packard, General Electric, Sprint, AT&T, and IBM. Outsourcing is not just for the private sector, however. Government agencies in forty states and Washington, D.C., use foreign workers to handle their customer service needs.

Tactical and Strategic Reasons for Outsourcing

Companies outsource for either tactical or strategic reasons. A decision to outsource is tactical when it aims to solve a practical problem—for example, when a company's staff is too small to handle the volume of work. That is a problem that can be solved by outsourcing. Outsourcing can be the answer to a variety of problems. A company may need to compete with larger firms by "beefing up" with virtual employees. It may need to get a specific task done but does not want to add more fixed costs to its overhead. A company may need the specialized and expensive tools of a contractor that it doesn't want to buy, store, maintain, and operate itself.

A decision to outsource is strategic when it is part of a company's long-term strategies, like repositioning itself in the marketplace. Early on, Coca-Cola Enterprises decided it did not have the capital, the time, or the expertise to efficiently produce its own bottles. So, it decided to license a group of bottle manufacturers to whom it sold its syrup concentrate. It follows a franchising model that outsources bottling to subsidiaries and to fully independent bottlers.

This was a strategic decision because it allowed Coca-Cola to expand its market by outsourcing a non-core business function, while maintaining its own focus on product quality and protecting its brand. Almost all of

Coca-Cola's supply chain is outsourced and the company is becoming a marketing organization that focuses on developing and branding new products, such as Diet Coke Plus (which contains vitamins) and Coca-Cola Zero (which is sugar- and calorie-free).

Outsourcing allows a U.S. company to benefit from another organization's skill, technology, and economies of scale.

We have already touched on outsourcing as a way to lower costs. Lowering costs obviously helps a company's bottom line when labor is cheaper outside of the United States. In India, for example, wages are 50–80 percent lower than those in the United States. But that isn't the only way costs can be reduced.

Outsourcing also allows a U.S. company to benefit from another organization's skill, technology, and economies of scale. The term "economies of scale" refers to savings that are made when unit costs (the price per item) go down as the volume of the merchandise produced increases. Those savings are passed on to the consumer in the form of cheaper cars, clothes, toys, and other merchandise.

An electronics manufacturing company named Flextronics Corporation makes the Xbox for Microsoft. Since Microsoft is primarily a software publisher, it would have had to build extensive manufacturing facilities capable of meeting a growing demand for the Xbox. By partnering with Flextronics, which is headquartered in Singapore, Microsoft was able to take advantage of that company's global manufacturing operations without investing in new plants. Thus, the two companies shared the risk and costs of producing the Xbox. Even with all its wealth, Microsoft couldn't have built all the factories it needed.

Outsourcing also gives a company access to experts who aren't available within the company, as can be seen in the Microsoft-Flextronics arrangement. Flextronics has design, engineering, manufacturing, and logistics operations in twenty-eight countries and has gained expertise that Microsoft could not hope to attain on its own.

Flexibility is another factor in a company's decision to outsource. For example, Coca-Cola Enterprises, which employs seventy-four thousand people in the United States, Canada, and Europe, had to address issues of service delivery and efficiencies in its employee benefits administration, which includes retirement and health care plans. Many of the company's business processes were highly decentralized, including human resources, which manages employee benefits. In the end, Coca-Cola decided to go with a combination of outsourcing and insourcing. Flexibility was a deciding factor: because Coca-Cola deals with two hundred unions and has to negotiate so many agreements with all of them, it needed the greatest freedom to strike the best deals possible with each union.

Microsoft's Xbox 360 is show-cased at the Tokyo Game Show. Microsoft partners with a global electronics manufacturer to produce this game console.

Boeing's Outsourcing Strategies

Often, there are multiple reasons for large companies or corporations to outsource. For a better understanding of this, let's look at the example of the aerospace giant Boeing. Boeing needed to cut costs to be able to compete against the more efficient Airbus, a European aerospace conglomerate that produces around 50 percent of the world's jet airliners. On one level, Boeing outsources for the same reasons as other companies. It uses Russian

Boeing used design and engineering talent from around the world to build its "green" passenger jet, the 787 Dreamliner, which has fuel-efficient design features.

engineers and Indian software technicians because of the inexpensive know-how they provide.

However, Boeing also looks to outsourcing to gain a competitive edge that is not about saving money. It recruits the most highly skilled workers, regardless of the cost. It also outsources to China and India to gain access to the largest, fastest-growing markets for aviation in the world. In exchange for the right to sell its planes in those markets, it is required to invest in manufacturing in those countries. This is known as an offset agreement.

In 2006, Boeing pursued design and engineering talent around the world for its 787 Dreamliner. It outsourced more than 70 percent of the 787's airframe, and gave all of its suppliers in Japan, Italy, and Russia the job of performing detail design of parts. "One of the things we have found [is that] it's best to have the people building the parts [also] designing the parts," said Michael Bair, Boeing's vice president in charge of the 787 program, in

BusinessWeek. By transferring certain creative tasks to a contractor, Boeing can focus on its strengths. While contractors build component parts, Boeing's in-house engineers can continue to create the conceptual design, technical requirements of the aircraft, and system architecture, as well as oversee the integration of parts and the testing and certifying of planes.

Considering Outsourcing Pros and Cons

According to Forrester Research, 88 percent of the firms they contacted said they got better value for their money overseas, and 71 percent said overseas workers did higher-quality work. On a national scale, economists have argued that by bringing down prices, outsourcing brings greater economic benefit to all. But the issue of how outsourcing affects the American economy is open to debate, as we will see in the next chapter.

In the end, it is up to each company to weigh the benefits of outsourcing against the obvious advantages of working with one's own employees, who have a better understanding of the core business and its strategies, customers, culture, and politics. After all, internal staff can offer continuity that a contractor, no matter how inexpensive and high-quality its services, cannot.

The Effects of Outsourcing and Global Free Trade

The practice of outsourcing has become the source of heated debate in the United States, especially whenever the economy takes a downturn. Essentially, there are two schools of thought regarding free trade practices such as outsourcing. Some believe that outsourcing raises the standard of living for Americans, while there are those who believe that outsourcing actually contributes to poverty in America. Which side you're on depends on what piece of the puzzle you're looking at. Unfortunately, the puzzle pieces consist of conflicting statistics and unreliable anecdotal accounts.

The Effects on Local Communities and Job Markets

Many people blame the country's unemployment rate on outsourcing and are alarmed at the projections that millions more jobs will be outsourced in the years to

Workers of Delphi Corporation, an auto supplier, and their supporters protest plans to slash jobs and wages and close many of its U.S. plants.

come. They warn that without stable, high-paying jobs in American communities, there will be less tax revenue to pay for the education, health, infrastructure, and Social Security systems.

The news media report on job losses on an almost-daily basis. As a result, Americans have become accustomed to thinking of devastated American towns at the mere mention of outsourcing. The negative effects on communities supported by jobs that were later transferred elsewhere are undeniable. Announcements of plant closings keep coming as companies shift their strategies to compete in a global market. The automobile industry is a case in point. In 2005, General Motors Corporation announced that it was closing nine plants in North America by 2008, eliminating thirty thousand jobs. In 2006, Ford Motor Company announced plans to close fourteen thousand plants in North America and cut between twenty-five thousand to thirty thousand jobs by 2012. From 1996 to 2006, some eighty communities across the United States lost more than a third of their auto manufacturing jobs.

It is worth repeating that not all outsourcing means jobs transferred overseas. One American community's loss can be another American community's gain. When Tellabs, Inc., a maker of fiber-optic network equipment, laid off 325 workers and closed its Bolingbrook, Illinois, plant, it sent the work to a supplier in San Jose, California.

The first American jobs to go at the dawn of the outsourcing era were manufacturing jobs largely in the "Rust Belt," which refers to the Northeastern and Midwestern states whose economies were based on heavy industry and manufacturing. Many business leaders and economists believed that by transferring low-paying, blue-collar jobs to developing nations, the United States would gain high-paying jobs in cutting-edge technology, allowing it to compete in the global economy.

New fears emerged as the outsourcing trend moved into the white-collar job category, however. The latest jobs to be outsourced overseas are high-value knowledge-based services requiring advanced degrees. Highly trained U.S. college students may find that they cannot find jobs after graduation or may have to expect lower salaries than offered in previous years. This is because technology companies such as Dell, Microsoft, Intel, Texas Instruments, and Motorola are developing research and design centers in China, Russia, and India, and hiring from the talented pool of engineers in those countries.

A poll conducted by the market research firm Zogby International in August 2004 found that 71 percent of American voters believed that outsourcing jobs overseas hurts the economy. Another 62 percent believed that the U.S. government should impose some legislative action against companies that transfer domestic jobs overseas, possibly in the form of increased taxes on companies that outsource.

International Trade Agreements vs. Protectionism

In order to protect their domestic industries from foreign competition, countries use tariff barriers, quotas, and sub-sidies. The United States, however, has mostly supported the liberalization of international trade since the end of

World War II and eliminated such artificial barriers in its belief that free trade is healthy for the economy.

The United States has pursued trade agreements with many countries in successive multilateral negotiations under the General Agreement on Tariffs and Trade (GATT) treaty and its successor, the World Trade Organization (WTO). The U.S. government has also negotiated numerous managed trade agreements. These include the North American Free Trade Agreement (NAFTA) and the Central America Free Trade Agreement (CAFTA) with El Salvador, Nicaragua, Honduras, Guatemala, and the Dominican Republic. It has also reached a number of bilateral agreements with Jordan, Israel, Chile, Colombia, Australia, Morocco, Malaysia, Thailand, and others.

Whenever the economic forecast is negative, there is renewed discussion of protectionism, which is the opposite of free trade. Protectionism calls for restrained trade between nations through tariffs and other trade barriers.

One complaint of protectionists is that tax incentives— that is, lower tax rates—are given to U.S. firms for shifting jobs overseas. In addition, some American companies avoid U.S. taxes altogether by moving their headquarters overseas to tax-free haven countries, like the Bahamas. In order to protect American jobs, protectionists suggest that these incentives and loopholes be removed. Responding to a National League of Cities questionnaire in 2004, former presidential candidate John Kerry said,

The North American Free Trade Agreement (NAFTA) allows for greater and easier flow of goods shipped across the borders of Mexico, the United States, and Canada.

"Companies move offshore simply to avoid paying American taxes, yet they still get all of the same benefits, including government contracts. We should penalize these companies and deny them government contracts."

Trade Is a Two-Way Street

There was a public outcry in March 2008 when the U.S. Air Force awarded a $35 billion airborne tanker contract to Europe's Airbus, instead of Boeing, the United States' second-largest defense contractor. The air force had reviewed bids from both companies but cited Airbus's advantages in "capability, past performance, cost, and refueling performance" for its decision, wrote Bill Rigby for Reuters.

On the surface, critics would seem to be justified in questioning the air force's decision. It gives the appearance that Europe is profiting off of American defense needs. There is also the issue of security: sensitive military designs would now be in the hands of foreigners. Yet, the government quickly sought to explain that these fears were baseless, as the contract would be executed by Airbus's U.S. subsidiary, Los Angeles, California–based Northrop Grumman Corporation in Mobile, Alabama. Northrop said that this would create about forty-eight thousand direct and indirect jobs in the United States, compared with forty-four thousand jobs that the Boeing plan would have created. Northrop would also perform the high-end avionics work, the most sensitive aspect of the contract, thus minimizing security concerns.

This illustrates that there are at least two sides to the outsourcing story. Although devastated factory towns and local economies make a dramatic media-friendly story, they may not paint a true picture of how outsourcing affects the national economy. Sometimes, as in the case of Anderson, Indiana, new jobs are created after old ones are gone. The town was left twisting in the wind when a major employer, General Motors, closed down its plants there. But in 2007, Nestlé Corporation opened a large factory in Anderson. In fact, studies show that outsourcing does not lead to net job losses. The household employment survey published by the Bureau of Labor Statistics (BLS) indicates that there are 1.9 million more Americans currently employed than there were in 2001, a total of 138.3 million workers.

Where are these newly created jobs coming from? In large part, they have come from insourcing, which means foreign companies investing in the American economy and building manufacturing plants and other facilities. So, in effect, Americans are benefiting from other nations' outsourcing practices. Outsourcing and insourcing are forms of international trade, and trade is a two-way street. Here is some data on insourcing from the Organization for International Investment, a nonprofit research group based in Washington, D.C.:

- Insourcing (jobs created by U.S. subsidiaries of foreign companies) employs 5.1 million Americans and supports an annual payroll of $335.9 billion.
- The average compensation per insourced worker is $66,042, which is 32 percent

higher than average compensation at U.S. companies.

- U.S. subsidiaries of foreign companies man-ufacture goods in America that are exported around the world, accounting for nearly 19 percent of all U.S. exports, or $169.2 billion.
- The federal income taxes paid by U.S. sub-sidiaries of foreign companies are increasing. In 2006, they paid $40.1 billion in taxes.

Foreign direct investment, which totaled $183.5 billion in 2006, also plays a major role in the U.S. economy, both as a key driver of the economy and as a source of inno-vation, exports, and jobs. U.S. exports grew 12 percent in 2007, providing a cushion against the painful housing downturn.

Furthermore, studies by the International Monetary Fund (IMF) have shown that an increase in outsourcing does not cause a slower rate of job growth. William T. Dickens, a professor at the University of Maryland School of Public Policy, and Stephen J. Rose, the author of *Social Stratification in the United States*, wrote, "The U.S. economy creates tens of millions of jobs every year, replacing the tens of millions of jobs that are lost due to the forces of competition and technical change." The reality of the global marketplace is that work is increasingly shared across borders.

The International Monetary Fund (IMF; www.imf.org) is an international organization established to promote monetary cooperation, foster economic growth and high levels of employment, and provide financial assistance to countries struggling with debt.

Distribution of Wealth

A fact that neither side disputes is that outsourcing generates huge profits for U.S. companies. This leads to higher stock prices in markets, argue supporters of free trade, and this, in turn, increases the wealth of the millions of Americans who own mutual funds or individual retirement accounts.

Nevertheless, one problem remains and it may be at the root of outsourcing fears: the uneven distribution of this income. In the current economy, people who work for wages and don't have an ownership stake in their company do not necessarily benefit when the company increases its profits. The answer, say many policymakers, is for the U.S. government not to become more protectionist but to adopt a more progressive federal tax system and increase investment in education and assistance for dislocated workers. For example, government programs that are currently offered to blue-collar workers who lose their jobs to foreign competition could be extended to white-collar workers as well. Public policies should support training, health insurance and pension portability, and unemployment compensation programs. When the economy is in a decline, however, there is a limit to what the government is willing to do.

The Trouble with Outsourcing

4

There are real problems associated with outsourcing. They fall into two categories: the practical and the ethical. An example of a practical problem in overseas outsourcing is the possibility of a culture clash. This can refer to corporate culture or the cultural differences of a foreign country. Corporate culture defines a company's personality and values. These values may be in-step with those of their host nation, or they may go against the grain of a country's sensibilities. An important step for a corporation interested in outsourcing some of its functions is to do an on-site visit. This provides an opportunity for the outsourcer to observe how employees interact with each other and with management. The outsourcer would also learn something about how employees approach and perform their work.

Other practical problems can be anticipated and addressed. It's obvious when there is a language barrier, and certain jobs, such as operating a call center, are not suitable to be outsourced where such a problem exists. Fortunately, English is widely spoken in many countries.

Culture Clashes

Cultural differences are trickier. U.S. companies have collided with culture shock in India and other countries. For example, Americans expect more independence and feedback from their workers. An American worker might change his or her approach to a task in order to meet a deadline, whereas an Indian worker perceives the way work is done to be more important and may stick to a rigid procedure, even if it means missing a deadline. "Americans in particular expect a lot more initiative, independent thinking, and pushback from their workers," said Mindy Blodgett, an analyst with the Yankee Group, a technology research and consulting firm, to *Network World*. Indians are more concerned with following the established steps in a process. In general, Americans don't worry about losing their job for contradicting their boss, but in India, employee outspokenness and input are not the cultural norm.

Another potentially significant cultural difference is that Americans don't need to like their coworkers or have personal relationships with them as long as they get the work done on time. In some countries, such as India, it's often much more about relationship building.

Some businesspeople will even make a deal with someone they know and trust without signing a contract, something that Americans would never do for fear of broken promises and subsequent lawsuits.

Experience shows that American managers who ignore cultural differences between the two workforces don't get the expected benefits, including cost savings. Cross-cultural training can help American companies teach onshore and offshore staff how to better collaborate and work toward common goals.

An emerging middle class of educated and computer-savvy professionals has led to an explosion in information technology, Internet services, and technology jobs in India.

Ethical Issues: Labor and the Environment

The ethical problems of outsourcing have to do with the bigger picture of free trade. Policies that support free trade frequently come into conflict with labor and environmental activists who are concerned that hard-won labor and environmental standards established in the United States do not have to be followed by overseas companies. They believe that outsourcing is a way for

U.S. corporations to avoid following these usually costly union and environmental requirements. Activists assert that trade agreements such as the WTO, which often view environmental protections as trade barriers, are a threat to these very protections and to the United States' ability to implement its own laws.

For instance, the WTO ruled that the U.S. Clean Air Act, which required that gasoline sold in the United States by domestic or foreign producers meet certain standards of cleanliness, was illegal. This ruling prevented the U.S. government from regulating third-party companies. The WTO also ruled the Endangered Species Act to be illegal.

Activists further assert that the WTO and other trade agreements undermine labor and environmental protections in favor of corporate gains. According to Global Exchange, a global trade watchdog, the WTO rules are written by and for corporations with inside access to negotiations, and consumer, environmental, human rights, and labor organizations are consistently ignored. Among its accusations is that the WTO hurts poor, small countries in favor of rich, powerful nations by leaving the former out of negotiations and creating a trade environment in which only the lowest wages can compete. Global Exchange also accuses the WTO of supporting child labor through its ruling that it is illegal for a government to ban a product based on the way it's produced. Another WTO ruling states that governments cannot take into account "non-commercial values" such as human rights when making purchasing decisions.

The International Labor Organization (ILO), a special-ized agency of the United Nations that deals with labor issues, estimates that there are 218 million child laborers between the ages of five and seventeen in the Asia-Pacific region, Sub-Saharan Africa, Latin America, and the Caribbean. In some cases, this refers to seventeen-year-olds helping out on the family farm. But what is alarming is that many children work long hours, often in dangerous and unhealthy conditions, and are often subject to physical abuse.

Without strict controls, globalization may be opening the door to cheap products at a terrible cost. For example, the Ivory Coast is the largest exporter of the world's cocoa beans and is also where the harvesting of cocoa beans is done by child slaves. Hershey's and M&M Mars, which dominate the $13 billion U.S. chocolate industry, are among those companies who have used large amounts of cocoa from the Ivory Coast. The U.S. State Department estimated that there are approximately fifteen thousand children working on cocoa, coffee, and cotton farms in the Ivory Coast. In its report "A Global Alliance Against Forced Labor" in 2005, the ILO estimated that at least 12.3 million people worldwide work as slaves or some other form of forced labor.

Cheap laborers—including child workers—from Mali and Burkina Faso contribute to the cocoa industry.

Even when it's not about slave labor, there are concerns that the low labor costs that are drawing jobs overseas are so low because there are no protections for workers there. If workers try to organize, then they get fired. Sometimes, they are even put in jail.

Of additional concern to labor activists is that corporations are being given huge tax breaks to take jobs overseas. The profits made overseas by U.S. companies are taxed at a lower rate than their U.S. income. In essence, the companies can hide their profits overseas.

This gives them greater incentive to build their factories in foreign countries. In 2005, Congress "decided to sweeten the deal for these corporate job exporters," wrote Senator Byron Dorgan in *Take This Job and Ship It*. A provision that was part of the JOBS (Jumpstart Our Business Strength) Act allowed companies to pay just 5¼ percent tax on any income they wanted to bring into the United States. Corporations brought back nearly $350 billion, which added up to a $104 billion tax break for them.

When Outsourcing Is Not the Answer

Nevertheless, outsourcing is not the answer for all businesses. Some companies discover that for them the problems outweigh the benefits, or that the anticipated benefits do not materialize. Financial advantages, for example, are reduced because of hidden costs. There are also non-financial costs, including lower customer approval and reduced morale and productivity from remaining domestic employees.

New Balance is the only shoe company that makes any athletic shoes in the United States and has five U.S. plants. It keeps 25 percent of its manufacturing domestic. In spite of labor costs that are ten to twelve times higher, New Balance's productivity is greater, which results in the lowering of other costs. It is able to deliver shoes

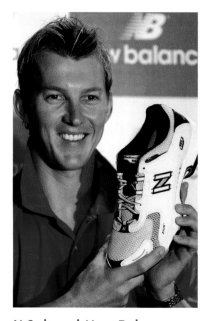

U.S.-based New Balance is able to deliver shoes more quickly than its competitors, which have to ship their products from overseas.

into the market in days, compared with weeks and sometimes months for its competitors—Nike, Adidas, and Reebok—which have to ship their product in from overseas.

North Fork Bank had its customer service call center in India, but there were problems. Customers complained that workers weren't familiar with geographic locations in the United States. When the bank's customer service representatives didn't know the difference between Southampton and Westhampton (both towns in Long Island, New York), it hurt its reputation as a neighborhood bank. So, these jobs were brought back to Long Island, even though it added $2 million a year in expenses.

Forces of Resistance

L oss of jobs to outsourcing has spurred American workers to demand protections from the U.S. government. In 2005, nearly all fifty U.S. states proposed legislation that would either prohibit or severely limit outsourcing. However, only a handful of these laws were passed. Most of these bills outlined restrictions on state contract work being done offshore and measures to limit the use of offshore call centers.

Bringing Jobs Back Home

Business leaders argue against this protectionist approach because it would harm the United States' competitiveness in the global market. They say that the United States should be more creative and nimble— global rather than protectionist. Limiting a company or organization from competition in a free market has proven to have adverse effects. In New Jersey in 2003, the state unemployment services hired a contractor for a call center, and that contractor used workers in India. This drew a lot of criticism, and in response, the state government brought more of these jobs back to New Jersey. As a result, New Jersey taxpayers paid, on top of the original contract costs, an additional $900,000 for the moving of twelve jobs back to the state. The move cost taxpayers more than $70,000 per job. "Saving" 1,400 domestic jobs in the future would cost the state an additional $100 million if New Jersey brought back a dozen call centers from India and Mexico.

Because government agencies are the biggest purchasers of goods of all kinds, there are concerns that political pressure to favor domestic suppliers over their foreign competitors can be very strong. Therefore, the United States, along with twenty-eight other nations, signed the WTO's Agreement on Government Procurement, which prohibits state and federal procurement policies from discriminating on the basis of where work will be performed. In spite of the WTO agreement, states such as New Jersey have taken steps to bring jobs back home.

Big Labor Weighs In

Often, unions mount the political pressure that the WTO's Agreement on Government Procurement tries to guard against. A trade or labor union is an organization

Members of the largest labor federation, the AFL-CIO, march in Boston, Massachusetts, in an effort to energize the labor movement.

of workers whose goal is to protect and advance the interests of its members, usually in the key areas of wages, hours, and work conditions. Today, most American labor unions are members of one of two labor federations: the American Federation of Labor and Congress of Industrial Organizations (AFL-CIO) and the Change to Win Federation, which broke away from the AFL-CIO in 2005.

Because outsourcing is seen as harmful to American workers (not to mention underpaid and overworked foreign workers who "benefit" from the outsourcing of

U.S. jobs), it is one of the issues taken on by the AFL-CIO and others. Union supporters assert that American employers have the power to prevent workers from joining unions by forcing workers to attend anti-union meetings during work hours and to meet with supervisors who deliver anti-union messages, for instance. Unions fear that at the expense of workers, the United States has spent too much to spur the economic development of other countries, building new factories on foreign land that are subsidized by loans, credits, and guarantees from the U.S. government, the World Bank, and the IMF.

Protectionist Legislation and Immigration Controls

Since January 2004, forty states have considered various anti-outsourcing bills. Most of these have been bans on foreign or out-of-state bidders competing for state contracts, the offering of preferences to American or in-state contractors competing for state projects, and the imposition of restrictions on certain fields such as call centers. Federal legislation has also been proposed to alter the tax code to discourage outsourcing and to place restrictions on those seeking foreign visas.

Recently, the debate over foreigners entering the United States to work has centered on a controversial work permit. The technology sector has long blamed counterproductive restrictions on immigration for forcing high-tech companies to outsource more jobs overseas. A few years ago, 195,000 H-1B visas were issued. But then a cap was placed, reducing that number to 65,000 a year.

In March 2008, Microsoft chairman Bill Gates testified before the U.S. Congress at a hearing on immigration reform. According to the *Seattle Post-Intelligencer*, he told Congress that its "failure to pass high-skilled immigration reform has exacerbated an already grave situation." He was referring to the limits on H-1B visas that do not take into account the U.S. economy's demand for skilled workers. All sixty-five thousand of the H-1B visas for fiscal year 2008 were snapped up in one day last April. Since then, employers have been waiting to apply for visas for fiscal year 2009. "Last year, for example, Microsoft was unable to obtain H-1B visas for one-third of the highly qualified foreign-born job candidates that we wanted to hire," Gates said. However, opponents say lifting the caps will take jobs from U.S. workers.

Protecting Foreign and Child Laborers

Another powerful force working against the most harmful effects of outsourcing and globalization operate from within corporate America. Concerns about companies' ethical conduct have created a growing trend: share-

Microsoft chairman Bill Gates asks the House Committee on Science and Technology to increase the number of visas that allow highly skilled foreigners to work in the United States in 2008.

holder activism. Since the 1970s, shareholders have pressured companies on a wide range of human rights and environmental issues. For example, a shareholder named Ray Rogers accused the Coca-Cola Company of violating human rights in Colombia at a shareholder meeting in 2004 and was forcibly removed from the building. He was referring to the case of a half-dozen union activists who worked at Coca-Cola bottling plants who had been murdered since 1989. A Colombian union sued Coca-Cola and its Colombian bottlers in U.S. courts.

Rogers has also encouraged student protests and the boycotting of Coke products.

Shareholder activism can play an important role in holding corporations accountable for their ethical behavior. Companies have been called to account for doing business under repressive regimes, like apartheid South Africa; creating oppressive and dangerous working conditions in factories; and causing a negative health or environmental impact through irresponsible practices.

Companies have an obligation to their shareholders, who may demand that they be socially responsible in running their operations. These same shareholders may put pressure on their boards of directors if they are against outsourcing. From the outcry against Nike's substandard wages for its Asian factory workers to Kathie Lee Gifford's clothing company's use of child labor, the issue of corporate social responsibility is part of the outsourcing debate. As part of its due diligence, a company that plans on outsourcing must make sure the contractor does not discriminate in hiring and promotion, pays its employees promptly and in full; and is environmentally responsible.

In the global market, the welfare of American workers must share the stage with the welfare of foreign workers. We have discussed forced labor and inadequate wages, but the fact of the matter is that globalization has improved the standard of living of millions of workers

No Sweat Apparel, a Massachusetts clothing company, challenges Nike to open its books on what it pays workers at the company's Asian factories.

around the world. In the Philippines, for example, cities such as Cebu, which attracts U.S. businesses with its infrastructure and workforce quality, can boast a 97 percent literacy rate and an excellent quality of life. This includes a cost of living that is 75 percent lower than in the United States. This, in turn, results in low employee turnover.

Myths and Facts

Myth: Outsourcing results in the loss of American jobs.

Fact: While outsourcing results in loss of some American jobs, the net rate of job loss since 2001 has actually decreased. Today, there are almost 2 million more Americans employed than there were in 2001.

Myth: Outsourcing means the exporting of American jobs, and American workers don't benefit from outsourcing.

Fact: Insourcing (jobs created by U.S. subsidiaries of foreign companies) employs 5.1 million Americans and supports an annual payroll of $335.9 billion. The average compensation per insourced worker is $66,042, which is 32 percent higher than average compensation at U.S. companies. U.S. subsidiaries of foreign companies manufacture goods in America that are exported around the world, accounting for nearly 19 percent of all U.S. exports, or $169.2 billion, raising more than $40 billion in taxes.

Myth: More American jobs are being outsourced—and lost—than are being gained or created.

Fact: According to the Organization for International Investment, a business association based in Washington, D.C., the numbers of manufacturing jobs insourced to the United States grew by 82 percent, while the number of jobs outsourced grew by only 23 percent.

Creating American Jobs and Planning for Tomorrow's Global Economy

Many problems have arisen from outsourcing, but does that mean outsourcing is the problem? Economists point out that free trade has brought millions of the jobs into the United States. But these jobs often do not directly replace lost jobs. Jobs close in one industry and open in another. Wealth is created, but the distribution of it is uneven. A town that is devastated because of plant closings will not necessarily be the recipient of new economic growth.

The solution to these kinds of economic dislocations requires a multi-pronged approach that includes improved education, retraining and financial support for displaced workers, and investments in jobs that cannot be outsourced offshore.

The Importance of Education

American schools are often criticized for not providing students with a strong enough grounding in science and math to keep them competitive in the global economy. For example, India graduates seventy-five thousand computer scientists a year, compared with only fifty-two thousand in the United States. It appears that colleges and universities have been slow to adapt to changing needs in different industries.

The salary for a programmer in India with two to three years of experience is one-eighth that of a programmer in the United States with similar skills and experience.

Jobs in the IT industry have been transferred to developing countries where well-educated employees work for lower wages. The salary for a programmer with two to three years of experience averages $7,500 in India. In Russia, it's $10,000, and in the United States, it's $65,000. It's not that all IT jobs are disappearing, but they are changing. The lower-end programming jobs, the call centers, system maintenance, and help desks are going offshore. IT workers with only technical knowledge are vulnerable to outsourcing. "But if you can combine business or scientific knowledge with technical savvy, there are a lot of opportunities [in the U.S.]," says Thomas Malone, author of *The Future of Work*.

"And it's a lot harder to move that kind of work offshore." Therefore, IT degree programs should incorporate broader business education, and students need to gain extra skills such as speaking a foreign language.

Insourcing: A Reverse Flow of American Jobs

As we discussed earlier, the number of jobs coming from overseas to the United States is growing faster than the jobs being outsourced. According to the Organization for International Investment, a business association based in Washington, D.C., the numbers of manufacturing jobs insourced to the United States grew by 82 percent, while the number of jobs outsourced grew by only 23 percent. Multinational corporations open offices on U.S. soil and pay American workers higher wages to do jobs that they once lured overseas. An example of this is a customer service call center in Reno, Ohio, with 250 workers answering phones for the online travel service Expedia. The Indian conglomerate Tata Group owns the center. Its American workers cost up to 40 percent more than their Indian counterparts. Why are Expedia and Tata willing to pay more for this labor that could be easily and cheaply outsourced? To provide their U.S. customers with a less frustrating customer service experience. They believe that happy customers will, in turn, lead to more business and higher profits, offsetting the higher wages.

According to the Organization for International Investment, firms headquartered abroad employ 5.1 million Americans in their U.S. offices. Typically, these jobs have been in manufacturing. Now, as more companies find distinct advantages in hiring Americans, the mix is changing. Lehui Enterprises, a Chinese condiment maker, invested $12 million to build a soy sauce factory outside Atlanta, Georgia. Wipro, an Indian IT services firm, is spending $150 million per office to open several software development offices in U.S. college towns in order to access the uniquely American innovation and entrepreneurship percolating there. Gruma, the world's largest tortilla maker, based in Mexico, invested $51.5 million to open a factory in Los Angeles, California, in 2008.

The Way Forward for American Workers and the U.S. Economy

However, scrambling for low-paying jobs in manufacturing and service industries is not the answer, says Richard Florida, author of *The Flight of the Creative Class*. Rather, the United States should reinvent itself to compete for high-paying jobs that require creativity and innovation, like knowledge-based jobs that range from architects, engineers, and scientists, to artists and writers, and encompassing the fields of health care, finance, and law. What drives economic growth, he argues, is the ability to

IBM joins forces with India's largest private telecom firm.

attract and retain talented people—not simply competing for goods, services, and capital. At present, roughly 30 percent (or forty million workers) of the American workforce uses its creativity at work, leaving the remaining 70 percent "holding on dearly to far lower-paying service or manufacturing jobs."

Some policymakers are looking to support education and training in emerging industries such as the green building industry. They predict that green building will create millions of construction, engineering, and architectural jobs relating to the retrofitting of twenty million homes to make them more energy efficient. These are exactly the kinds of creative jobs that Richard Florida writes about, the kind that cannot be exported.

James Flanigan, a senior economics editor for the *Los Angeles Times*, looks at the outsourcing dilemma in this way: "We've been here before. In the 1960s, the anxiety was over computers idling millions of workers. In the 1980s, the rise of Japanese industry was supposed to turn Americans into hamburger flippers. The nightmare visions didn't come true then, and they certainly won't come true today. Computers unleashed a huge new information industry, creating many thousands of jobs. And the competition from Japan pushed America into new frontiers such as technology and health care, where the U.S. now dominates."

The outsourcing of U.S. jobs is not necessarily the problem, and other countries' hard workers are not the enemy. What the United States should really be concerned with is declining educational performance, especially in math and science, and a resulting future deficit in tech-nological and intellectual ingenuity and innovation. It is innovation, skill, and know-how that have allowed the United States to become a world leader over the past hundred years. If it hopes to stay in front of the global pack, then its commitment to fostering an educated, intelligent, hard-working, and creative citizenry must not slacken, but in fact be strengthened. If the United States is to create jobs, services, and products that are so specialized, advanced, high quality, and unique that they can be supplied by no other nation, then it must invest in its citizens. It must create the kind of people who provide a return on that investment, who will think creatively, dream big, and work hard to achieve prosperity for themselves and for their country.

Glossary

activism The practice of taking direct, militant action to achieve a political or social goal, sometimes by demonstrations and protests.

domestic Produced in or concerning a particular country.

federation An organization formed by several groups, such as nations, states, societies, or unions, each keeping control of its own internal affairs.

free trade Principles of international trade that is free of government interference.

globalization Growth to a global or worldwide scale, especially in business.

information technology (IT) The study, design, development, support, or management of computer-based information systems, mainly software applications and computer hardware.

insourcing The business practice of using a company's own personnel and resources; also, of transferring jobs within the country.

liberalization The practice of becoming less strict.

nearshore outsourcing The business practice of transferring jobs to a neighboring country.

offshoring The business practice of transferring jobs to a foreign country.

outsourcing The act of obtaining goods or services from a supplier outside of the company or the country.

quota A limitation, as on imports.

regime A government in power.

subsidize To support through grants (subsidies) paid by the government.

tariff A government tax on imports or exports.

tax code A body of tax law, usually covering income taxes, payroll taxes, gift taxes, estate taxes, etc.

union An organization of employees formed to gain and exert bargaining power over an employer and to protect employees from exploitation, abuse, and mistreatment.

For More Information

American Federation of Labor-Congress of Industrial
    Organizations (AFL-CIO)
815 16th Street NW
Washington, DC 20006
Web site: http://www.aflcio.org
The AFL-CIO is a voluntary federation of fifty-six national
    and international labor unions representing 10.5
    million members.

Brookings Institution
1775 Massachusetts Avenue NW
Washington, DC 20036
(202) 797-6000
Web site: http://www.brookings.edu
Brookings Institution is a nonprofit public policy
    organization whose goal is to promote a strong
    U.S. democracy and foster economic and social
    welfare, security, and opportunity for all
    Americans, and a more open, safe, and cooperative
    international system.

Conference Board of Canada
255 Smyth Road
Ottawa, ON K1H 8M7

Canada
(866) 711-2262
Web site: http://www.conferenceboard.ca
This Canadian organization specializes in economic
trends, public policy, and organizational performance.

World Trade Organization (WTO)
Centre William Rappard
Rue de Lausanne 154
CH-1211 Geneva 21
Switzerland
Tel: (41-22) 739 51 11
Web site: http://www.wto.org
The WTO is the only global international organization
dealing with the rules of trade between nations.

Web Sites

Due to the changing nature of Internet links, Rosen
Publishing has developed an online list of Web sites
related to the subject of this book. This site is updated
regularly. Please use this link to access this list:

http://www.rosenlinks.com/itn/ousj

For Further Reading

Daniels, Kathryn. *Common Sense Business for Kids*. Placerville, CA: Bluestocking Press, 2005.

Florida, Richard. *The Flight of the Creative Class: The New Global Competition for Talent*. New York, NY: Collins, 2007.

Friedman, Thomas L. *The World Is Flat: A Brief History of the Twenty-First Century*. New York, NY: Farrar, Straus & Giroux, 2005.

Gilman, Laura Anne. *Economics* (How Economics Works). Minneapolis, MN: Lerner, 2006.

Greaves, Bettina Bien. *Economics: A Free Market Reader*. Placerville, CA: Bluestocking Press, 2005.

Hess, Karl. *Capitalism for Kids: Growing Up to Be Your Own Boss*. Placerville, CA: Bluestocking Press, 2005.

Marks, Gene. *The Complete Idiot's Guide to Successful Outsourcing*. New York, NY: Alpha Books, 2005.

van Agtmael, Antoine. *The Emerging Markets Century: How a New Breed of World-Class Companies Is Overtaking the World*. New York, NY: Free Press, 2007.

Williams, Jane A. *Economics* (A Bluestocking Guide). Placerville, CA: Bluestocking Press, 2004.

Bibliography

Associated Press. "GM Slashing 30,000 Jobs, Closing Plants." MSNBC.com. November 21, 2005. Retrieved March 12, 2008 (http://www.msnbc.msn.com/id/10138507).

Buchholz, Todd G. *Bringing the Jobs Home*. New York, NY: Sentinel, 2004.

Cook, John, and Paul Nyhan. "Outsourcing's Long-Term Effects on U.S. Jobs at Issue." *Seattle Post-Intelligencer*, March 10, 2004. Retrieved February 22, 2008 (http://seattlepi.nwsource.com/business/164018_outsource10.asp).

Dorgan, Byron L. *Take This Job and Ship It*. New York, NY: Thomas Dunne Books, 2006.

Dubie, Denise. "Offshoring." Network World, February 8, 2008. Retrieved February 21, 2008 (http://www.networkworld.com/news/2008/020808-offshoring.html).

Fisher, Anne. "Worried About Outsourcing? Cheer 'Insourcing.'" CNNMoney.com, October 24, 2006. Retrieved February 23, 2008 (http://money.cnn.com/2006/10/23/news/economy/insourcing.fortune/index.htm).

Flanigan, James. "Globalization Is Doing a World of Good for U.S." *Los Angeles Times*, April 24, 2005.

Retrieved March 15, 2008 (http://www.rutledgecapital. com/pdf_files/20050424_latimes_flanigan_global.pdf).

Florida, Richard. *The Flight of the Creative Class*. New York, NY: Collins, 2007.

Franklin, James C. *Employment Outlook 2006–16*. U.S. Department of Labor, Bureau of Labor Statistics, November 2007. Retrieved February 23, 2008 (http:// www.bls.gov/opub/mlr/2007/11/art1full.pdf).

Frauenheim, Ed. "Study: States Doing Plenty of Offshoring." CNetNews.com, July 14, 2004. Retrieved March 10, 2008 (http://www.news.com/Study-States-doing-plenty-of-offshoring/2100-1022_3-5269261.html).

Hira, Ron, and Anil Hira. *Outsourcing America*. New York, NY: Amacom, 2005.

Holmes, Stanley. "Boeing's Global Strategy Takes Off." Businessweek.com, January 30, 2006. Retrieved March 11, 2008 (http://www.businessweek.com/ magazine/content/06_05/b3969417.htm).

Malone, Thomas W. *The Future of Work*. Cambridge, MA: Harvard Business School Press, 2004.

McDougall, Paul. "Airbus Deal Critics Ignore Boeing's Outsourcing." InformationWeek.com, March 12, 2008. Retrieved March 12, 2008 (http://www.informationweek. com/blog/main/archives/2008/03/airbus_deal_cri.html).

O'Brien, Jeffrey M. "The Making of the Xbox." *Wired*, November 2001. Retrieved March 12, 2008 (http:// www.wired.com/wired/archive/9.11/flex.html).

Prah, Pamela M. "States Stung by Work Sent Overseas." Stateline.org, August 11, 2004. Retrieved March 10, 2008 (http://www.stateline.org/live/ViewPage.action?siteNodeId=136&languageId=1&contentId=15734).

Press Trust of India. "Tight U.S. Immigration Forces Outsourcing: Gates." NDTVProfit.com, March 12, 2008. Retrieved March 12, 2008 (http://www.ndtvprofit.com/2008/03/12233715/Tight-US-immigration-forces-ou.html).

Reuters. "Boeing to Appeal $35 Billion Airbus Air Force Contract." InformationWeek.com, March 11, 2008. Retrieved March 12, 2008 (http://www.information-week.com/news/showArticle.jhtml;jsessionid=WUQGYKW02SILGQSNDLPSKH0CJUNN2JVN?articleID=206902897).

Rossi, Sandra, and Helen Schuller. "Outsourcing—Debating the Pros and Cons." *Computerworld*, April 24, 2006. Retrieved February 3, 2008 (http://computerworld.co.nz/news.nsf/mgmt/C9FF3337FE95F2D5CC2571570019892C).

van Agtmael, Antonine. *The Emerging Markets Century*. New York, NY: Free Press, 2007.

Yang, Jia Lynn. "Indian Call Center Lands in Ohio." *Fortune*, August 3, 2007. Retrieved February 19, 2008 (http://money.cnn.com/magazines/fortune/fortune_archive/2007/08/06/100141303/index.htm).

Index

About the Author

Jacqueline Ching is a writer who has written for *Newsweek* and the *Seattle Times*. She has written several books for Rosen Publishing related to history, society, human rights, and public policy, including *Abigail Adams: A Revolutionary Woman*; *The Assassination of Martin Luther King Jr.*; and *Women's Rights*.

Photo Credits

Cover (top left, top right), pp. 4, 5, 12, 13, 15, 18, 48, 49, 52 © AFP/Getty Images; cover (bottom), pp. 31, 33, 36, 38, 39, 41, 43 © Getty Images; pp. 7, 10, 17, 20, 21, 25, 44, 46 © AP Photos.

Designer: Tom Forget; Photo Researcher: Marty Levick